Surfing Lingo

A Dictionary of Surfing Terms

1st Edition

David Tuffley

To my beloved Nation of Four
Concordia Domi – Foris Pax

"Out of water, I am nothing."
Duke Kahanamoku

1st Edition Published 2015 by Altiora Publications
AltioraPublications.com/

ISBN-13: 978-1517588083 ISBN-10: 1517588081

About the Author
David Tuffley is a local from Australia's Gold Coast/Brisbane for nearly 60 years at time of writing. Surf culture is some of David's earliest memories; he still remembers like it was yesterday having his first Neptune's Cocktail and Sand Facial while learning how to surf. He gets back to the beach every chance he gets. Swimming in the ocean and surfing the waves is one of life's great pleasure.

www.facebook.com/tuffley/

Acknowledgements
My brother Steve, my father Alex and all the beach dudes I knew growing up.

Contents

Surfing Lingo: A Dictionary of Surfing Terms

Introduction

Riding waves has been part of Polynesian culture in the Western Pacific for centuries. It is not known exactly where and when it started, much less by whom. It may have been as simple as seeing dolphins surfing the breakers, something they do instinctively and appear to enjoy.

We do know that in 1767, the English navigator and explorer Samuel Wallis saw men surfing when he visited Tahiti. A few years later in 1778, another Englishman, James Cook saw the locals surfing the waves in Hawaii. Surfing was a good idea whose time had come; with more people visiting from Europe and America, the idea was sure to spread to the rest of the world eventually.

And spread it did; in 1907, Henry Huntington visited Hawaii on holiday and saw an opportunity to market his property interests in Redondo Beach California. Huntington hired a young Hawaiian, George Freeth (father was Irish) to come to Redondo and show everyone just how much fun it could be to ride the waves. The strategy worked spectacularly. Today, Huntington Beach, also known as HB and Surf City is an important center of Californian surfing culture.

3

In the Summer of 1914/15, another Hawaiian, Duke Kahanamoku came to Australia on a similar mission as Freeth. After putting on a series of successful display events at Freshwater Beach in Sydney, the Duke made his way north to the Gold Coast, surfing at Snapper Rocks, what is now part of the so-called *Superbank,* one of the longest point breaks in the world.

From its origins in Hawaii and its spread to the beaches of California and Australia, surfboard riding has become a global sport, as well as a lifestyle and occupation for millions of fun-loving thrill-seekers around the world.

In those early days, surfboards were big hardwood planks, 5 meters long (16 feet) and weighing as much as some adults. A replica of Kahanamoku's Australian board weighs 38 kgs (85 lbs). Board designs were bound to change over time as surfer's worked out better and better designs. It started with Freeth in California who cut the heavy board in half and shaped it down to make it more agile. Wood eventually gave way to fiberglass, fin designs improved, leg-ropes came into widespread use and a host other improvements.

Surfing Culture

Like any interest group with dedicated members, over time surfing has evolved its own sub-culture, including its own lexicon of colloquial expressions.

This book is a combination of Hawaiian-American and Australian surfing lingo; the two dominant surfing influences. While distinct these have much in common.

Some surfing expressions have found their way into popular culture; words like *awesome* and *dude* can be heard spoken naturally thousand miles from the nearest beach. The 'California Surfer-Dude' stereotype has earned its place in popular culture, as seen in the Simpson's character *Snake Jailbird*.

A Surfer's Code

Tempers have been known to flare when surfers don't follow a few simple, common-sense rules:

Don't drop in. Wait for your turn in the line-up and don't jump the queue. The person closest to the breaking wave has the right of way. Once on a wave, don't turn back until you are clear of the pack.

Be clear about your intentions. When starting out on a wave, let the surfers around you know which way you intend going.

Keep your board under control. Learn to roll over with your board as you duck under on-coming waves. Avoid throwing your board. The wind could take it and hurt someone. Your leg-rope and ankle strap should be in good condition, not likely to give way under pressure.

Paddle out around the side. Avoid paddling back out through the busy area where the waves are breaking and people are surfing. A rider on a wave always has right of way, so stay out of their way when paddling back out.

Respect your fellow surfers, the ocean and the beach. Watch them and learn from the more experienced surfers. Try not to get in their way. Do what you can to keep the ocean and the beach clean.

Surfing Terms A to Z

180 or **360**: A 180° or 360° aerial turn.

A

A-Frame: Premium surf; a barrel resembling an A-frame cross-section.

Aerial: Surfer and board breaks free of the water and is airborne for a time.

Aggro: Aggressive attitude.

Air: Getting momentum from a fast bottom turn, going up the face then flying off the lip, airborne for a time.

Akaw!: Old School exclamation for seeing a perfect wave.

Amped: Excited by great surfing, or the anticipation of great surfing; overdoing it.

Anglin': Turning left or right on a wave.

Ankle Busters / Snappers: Small waves no higher than one's ankles; useless for surfing.

Avalanche: An outer reef surf location off Oahu, Hawaii; where the white water pours down the face of a wave like snow in an avalanche.

Awesome: Great; fantastic.

B

Backdoor: Coming into the barrel from *behind* the peak of the breaking wave.

Back Down: To decide not to take off on a wave after all. You were going to, but thought better of it.

Backside: When a surfer's usual stance is reversed, for example when a regular-footed surfer (left foot to the front) reverses to put their right foot to the front, or vice versa.

Baggys/Baggies: Loose fitting swim shorts worn by surfers. Baggies come in a wide variety of colors and styles.

Bail: To bail out of a worsening situation by jumping off the board just ahead of being wiped out.

Banks: Sand bank near the shore that causes a beach break. The size and shape of the sand bank determines the quality of the wave.

Banzai: A yell of triumph by surfers as they ride a great wave.

Banzai Pipeline: Surfing location on the North Shore of Oahu, Hawaii, between Waimea Bay and Sunset Beach.

Barney: An inexperienced or incompetent surfer.

Barrel: When a curling wave is breaking perfectly, it creates a barrel-shaped hollow; also known as the *tube* or the *green room*.

Bottom turn: The turn at the bottom of the wave.

Beach bunny: Girls who hang-out at the beach.

Beach break: A fast, steep wave breaking close to the shore. Beach breaks are fun to ride, but are short-lived, closing lose-out completely as they finish. Good for beginners.

Beached: The feeling of being completely full after a big meal, as in too full to go surfing, have to stay on the beach.

Beach Leech: Someone who takes advantage of the generosity of other surfers to borrow a board, wax etc; a parasite.

Beaver tail: A wet suit with a detachable crotch piece that happens to be shaped like a beaver's tail.

Bell's Beach: Good surfing location in Victoria, Australia.

Benny: An outsider or stranger.

Big Gun: A long board designed for big waves; 9 foot or longer.

Bitchin': Old school term for excellent or enjoyable (also *Boss, Excellent, Primo, Rad*).

Black Beach: Good surfing location in San Diego, California.

Blank: The block from which a surfboard is made.

Blown out: Strong wind making the waves unrideable.

Boardies: Or board shorts; knee-length quick drying shorts worn by surfers in climates where wet-suits are not required.

Board: Surfboard.

Body Surfing: Riding waves with one's body; the body surfer makes their body stiff and rides the wave head first with arms held tight against their side, head slightly raised to see where they are going.

Bogus: False; lame; ridiculous; unbelievable.

Bomb: Unusually large set wave.

Bombora / Bommie: An Australian term for a wave breaking over an off-shore reef; often well outside the normal lineup.

Bone Yard: The wave break zone.

Booger / Boogieboarder: Body boarder (see Boogie board).

Boogie board: A short, soft board invented in the 1970's.

Boost: to become airborne from the lip of a wave.

Boss: Outstanding; excellent.

Bottom Turn: Making a turn at the base of the wave.

Bowl: a shallower section of sea-bed in the path of the wave that makes the wave break faster and harder.

Brah: Hawaiian term for surfer friend.

Breaker: A breaking wave.

Breakwater: A construction of rocks, concrete or other materials used to reduce beach erosion. Breakwaters absorb the energy of the incoming waves.

Bro: Brother.

Bubble (The): Good surfing location in Fuerteventura, Canary Islands.

Bummer: Too bad; a total drag; now in common usage.

Bundoran Beach: Good surfing location in County Donegal, Ireland.

Bunny: Beach girl, as in *Beach Bunny*.

Bureligh Heads: Good surfing location on the Gold Coast, Australia.

C

Carve / Carving: Cutting a path across or through a wave, done by performing a radical turn.

Caught inside: Trapped inside the line of breaking waves; being unable to get out to where the action is.

Channel: Sea-bed is deeper and the waves do not break. A breaking wave can peter out when it crosses a channel.

Charging: Riding a wave hard, aggressively.

Cheater Five: Getting five toes on the nose of the board; a move accomplished by squatting down, putting your weight on the back foot to keep balance, and extending the other foot forward.

Chinese Wax Job: Putting wax on the *bottom* of the board.

Choka: Really good, excellent.

Choppy, chop: When a strong cross-wind creates a rough surface on a wave. Chop makes the wave break unevenly and so is difficult to ride.

Chowder: Pollution or other undesirable substance(s) in the water.

Clamshell: When the lip of the wave comes down suddenly and engulfs the surfer. The lip on a good wave will descend more slowly, allowing the surfer to stay clear.

Clean: A wave that breaks from a single peak along its entire length; the surfer has an open face to ride across.

Clean Up Set: Larger than average wave or set of waves that break seaward of the line (of surfers waiting for a wave). The line is said to be dispersed, or *cleaned-up*.

Clidro: Turning up and down the face of a wave.

Climbing: Carving an S-shaped path on a wave.

Close-out: When a wave breaks all at once, making it impossible to ride.

Cloudbreak: Good surfing location in Tavarua Island, Fiji.

Cloud Nine: Good surfing location on Siargao Island, Philippines.

Clucked: Afraid of being out among the waves.

Coffin: Riding a board lying on your back, arms folded across the chest.

Corduroy: When a series of approaching swells form a corduroy-like pattern of lines when seen from a distance.

Cowabunga: Exclamation of triumph or surprise.

Cranking: When the conditions are good or excellent.

Crest: Top of the wave.

Cross Step / Stepping: A longboard maneuver where the rider walks down and back along the length of the board.

Cruncher: A hard-breaking wave that collapses on itself; an unridable wave.

Curl: The cascading part of the wave; the curl forms one half of the 'barrel' or 'green room', the other half by the face of the wave.

Cut-back: 180° turn; turning toward the breaking part of the wave.

Cut out: Exit the wave.

D

Dawn Patrol: Early morning surfing.

Deck: Top surface of the surfboard.

Desert Point: Good surfing location in Western Australia.

Ding: Damage to the surface of the board, though not serious enough to make the board unserviceable.

Dirty Lickings: Down and dirty from a wipeout.

Doggers: Colorful swimming trunks.

Dork: Socially inept person.

Double Spinner: Performing two complete turns in the one move.

Drop (or Taking the Drop): Coming down the face of the wave just after taking off. The initial plunge before reaching the bottom.

Drop in: To take off on a wave already claimed by another surfer; a move guaranteed to enrage the surfer being dropped in on; bad manners.

Drop Knee: Way of riding a longboard with one knee on the deck.

Dropping: Reaching the crest then cutting back to drop down again; done multiple times on the same wave.

Duck dive: Pushing the nose of the board underwater just before an on-coming wave, diving under to get past the wave.

Dude: A general purpose greeting, similar to 'man' or 'mate'. Can simply be a friendly form of address, or can be inflected in many ways to have a wide variety of meanings. Feminine form 'dudette'.

Dumping: Wave breaks along its length instead of progressively, impossible to ride.

Duranbah: Good surfing location on the Gold Coast, Australia.

Dweeb: A boring, stupid or socially inept person.

E

Eating It: Getting wiped-out, maybe getting water and sand forced into nose and mouth.

El Rollo: A 360 degree roll done by lying flat on the board, holding on to both rails, and rolling.

El Zonte: Good surfing location in El Salvador.

Endless Summer: Classic surf movie (1966), a source of inspiration for generations of surfers. If you have the resources you can follow the Summer around the world, visiting great surfing spots. The Endless Summer is what it might be like to die and go to surfer heaven.

Epic: Excellent surfing conditions.

Eskimo Roll: Rolling over as a wave approaches so the breaking wave hits the underside of the board. The rider then completes the roll and carries on out back.

Express Point: Good surfing location in Victoria, Australia.

F

Face: That part of the wave where the lip curls over.

Fade: When the surfer takes-off on a wave, turning initially towards the breaking part of the wave, then turning sharply away in the direction of break.

Fakie: To ride the board backwards, tail-first.

FCS: Fin Control System; a fin that can be unscrewed for travel, and/or easy replacement (no re-glassing required).

Fer Sure: For sure, as in *ok fine, fer sure, fer sure.*

Fetch: How far the wind travels across the water.

Fins-free snap: A top-of-the-wave turn where the fin slides off the top.

Fin: The downwards projecting piece at the tail that helps with directional stability.

Firing: Great surfing conditions.

Fish: A shorter, thicker board useful for surfing smaller waves.

Flat: Absence of waves.

Floater: Being on top of a breaking wave and coming down.

Foamies: A beginner's surfboard made of foam.

Foil: The cross-sectional profile of a board; thinner at the nose, becoming thicker towards the tail.

Froth: The white foam of a breaking wave.

Frube: A person who paddles out, but does not surf.

Funboard: A mid-sized surfboard.

G

Gas chamber: The tubular, slightly pressurized space created by a breaking wave where the surfer tries to ride without being wiped-out by getting too far in.

Geek: Someone who acts an inappropriate or socially awkward manner..

Gidget: A small female surfer, a contraction of 'girl midget'. Based on the lead character of Frederick Kohner's 1957 novel, *Gidget, the Little Girl with Big Ideas*.

Glasshouse: The tubular, slightly pressurized space created by a breaking wave. Similar to *Gas Chamber* and *Green Room*.

Glass Job : Descriptive of a surfboard's fiberglass finish.

Glassy: Smooth, clean surf occurring when there is little or no wind.

Gnarlatious: Really good, awesome.

Gnarly: A wave with a high degree of difficulty; a term now in common usage meaning anything difficult or dangerous.

Goat Boat: Water-craft that is *not* a surfboard; includes kayaks, surf-skis (aka wave skis). Hence a *goat-boater*.

Going off: Excellent surf, as in *it was going off this morning*.

Goofy foot: A board-rider who places their right foot forward.

Green Room: The tubular, slightly pressurized space created by a breaking wave. Similar to *Gas Chamber* and *Glass House*.

Gremlin: A beginner. Similar to *Grommet/Grom*.

Grey Belly: A big-bellied surfer with grey hair.

Grommet: A beginner.

Grom: A beginner.

Ground Swell: Bigger than normal swells caused by off-shore storms.

Grubbing: Falling off your board while riding a wave.

Gun: a thin surfboard between 6 to 10 feet in length. A design well-suited for big-wave riding.

H

Hang Heels: A backwards-facing stance with the heels hanging over the edge; only possible on a longboard.

Hang Eleven: When a guy surfs in the nude.

Hang-five/hang ten: A forwards-facing stance with five or ten toes hanging over the nose; only possible on a longboard.

Hairy: Difficult or dangerous conditions, similar to *gnarly*.

Hang loose: Relax, chill-out. Can be signaled with a thumb and pinkie up hand-wave.

Haole: Old Hawaiian term for pale-skinned Europeans.

Head Dip: Riding a wave and having your head come in contact with the water.

Headstand: Riding a wave while standing on your head.

Heavies: Big waves; anything bigger than 10 feet.

Hit the Surf. Go surfing.

Hodad: A wannabe surfer; someone who turns up at the beach and goes through the motions, but is not for real.

Hollow: A tubular wave.

Honeys: Women or girls, either surfers themselves or girlfriends of surfer.

Honker: A big wave, similar to *heavy*.

Hossegor: Good surfing location in France.

Hot-Dogging: Highly skilled moves performed by an experienced surfer.

Huarache Sandals: Sandals with tire-tread soles.

I

Impact Zone: Wave break zone; where the action is.

In the Soup: Being in the foam behind the breaking wave.

Indo: Indonesia.

Inside: Zone between the shore and the line-up; as distinct from *outside* where you catch a wave.

Instinct: Brand of surf gear.

J

Jeffrey's Bay / J Bay: Good surfing location in South Africa renowned for high-quality right-handers.

Jetty: Protruding man-made structure; breakwater.

Joe's Point: Good surfing location in Sur, Oman.

Junkyard Dog: Surfer of lesser ability; or someone who surfs in poor conditions.

K

Kahuna: In Hawaiian culture, Kahuna is a priest, sorcerer, magician, wizard, minister; an expert in any field. In surfing culture, Kahuna has come to mean the god of sun, sand, and surf.

Kamikaze: Rider stands at the nose holding their arms horizontally out.

Keg: Barrel of the wave; the tube.

Kick Out : Way of finishing a ride by turning back over the top of the wave.

Kickflip: When board and rider get airborne, and rider kicks the board to make it do a 360° rotation on it long axis, then landing back on it, right way up to continue on the wave.

Kirra: Good surfing location on the Gold Coast, Australia.

Knee boarding: Riding by kneeling on a short board.

Knots: Rough skin on the knees and feet built up by kneeling on a board.

Kook: A beginner; someone who does not observe surfing protocol.

L

Layback: Laying down flat on back while riding a wave.

Leash: Tether to keep board and rider together after a wipe-out. Velcro strap goes around the surfer's ankle, the other end attaches to the tail of the board.

Left: Looking towards the beach from outside, a wave that breaks from right to left.

Leg rope: As *Leash*.

Leggy: As *Leash*.

Lennox Head: Good surfing location in New South Wales, Australia.

Les Cavaliers: Good surfing location in Anglet, France.

Lima: Good surfing location in Peru

Line Up: Place just beyond the breakers where surfers wait for a wave.

Lines: Lines of unbroken waves moving towards the beach; swells before they break.

Lip: Foremost part of the breaking wave

Locked In: Riding with the tail of the board set firmly in the wave, holding it down.

Log: Wooden surfboard; pre-dating fiberglass boards.

Longboard: Round-nosed, 8 – 10 foot (3 meter) board.

Lull: Period of calm between sets.

M

Macker: Big wave; big enough to drive a Mack truck through.

Mal / Malibu: Longboard.

Man in Grey Suit: Shark.

Manu Bay: Good surfing location in New Zealand.

Margaret River: Good surfing location in Western Australia.

Mavericks: Good surfing location in California; known for big waves.

Max Out: Over the limit.

Meatball: *No Surfing* or *Beach Closed* flag.

Mentawai Islands: Good surfing location in Indonesia.

Messy: Untidy, closed-out surf.

Mondo: Epic proportions.

Montanita: Good surfing location in Ecuador.

Mullering: Severe wipe-out, damaging.

Mush / Mushy: Poor quality surf.

N

Narrabeen: Good surfing location in New South Wales, Australia.

Nailed: Getting wiped out.

Neptune Cocktail: Seawater swallowed during a wipeout.

New School: Recent generation of surfer, particularly ones who perform tricks.

Noah: Shark, as in *Noah's Ark*.

Noodled: One's arms very tired, being as strong as a wet noodle.

Noosa Heads: Good surfing location in Queensland, Australia.

Nose: Forward-most tip of the board.

O

Offshore: Wind blowing offshore, away from the beach; usually makes for good surfing conditions.

Off the hook: Waves are good, conditions favorable.

Off the Richter: Very good, as in better than 10 out of 10, the limit of the Richter Scale of earthquake magnitude.

Off the Top: Carving turn at the top of a wave.

Off the Wall: Very good, as in *off the Richter, awesome.*

Onshore Winds: Wind that blows onshore, towards the beach; creates unfavorable surfing conditions.

Out Back: Beyond the breaking waves; where you wait for a wave.

Outrageous: Very good, as in *off the Richter, off the wall, awesome.*

Outside: Beyond the breaking waves; where you wait for a wave.

Outside Break: The furthest point from the beach where waves are breaking. Surfers watch this space for waves that break unusually far out.

Overhead: Wave taller than a standing surfer.

Over the falls: Sucked up and over a breaking wave after falling off the board.

P

Paddle puss: Timid or indifferent surfer staying close to the beach.

Pambula Rivermouth: Good surfing location in New South Wales, Australia.

Party Wave: Multi-rider wave.

Pendleton: Colorful shirt, named after surf location north of San Diego, California.

Pearl: Burying the nose of the board in the water causing a rapid slow-down and forward tumble, as in *pearl diving*.

Pit: In front of the breaking wave; the place you hit when you wipeout.

Pitched: Flung off the lip of the wave.

Pipeline: Good surfing location on the North Shore of Oahu, Hawaii. Not for beginners.

Playa Naranjo: Good surfing location in Costa Rica, also *Potrero Grande.*

Pocket: Space below the curving lip of the wave.

Point break: Off-shore from a headland or point where the shoaling seabed causes waves to break; usually good for surfing.

Pop-Out: Mass produced surf-board.

Pop-up: Smooth movement of standing up on a board from a lying position.

Poser: Someone pretending to be a surfer.

Pounder: Powerful, hard-breaking wave.

Priority: Person with right-of-way on a wave.

Prone: Laying flat on a board.

Primo: Excellent, number one.

Prone Out: Pulling off a wave by lying down on the board; nose digs in and the tail flips around.

Pull Out: Turning back, up and through a wave to end a ride.

Pump: When a surfer generates more speed by rhythmically pushing down on the board with their feet. Pushing the board down into the water, the buoyancy effect makes it spring forwards on the upstroke.

Pumping: Good surfing conditions. Also the act of getting more speed.

Q

Quiksilver: Australian brand of surfing merchandise.

Quiver: Surfer's collection of boards.

Quasimoto: Hunched over posture, crouching on the nose.

R

Radical / Rad: Extreme in a good sense; very good, as in *boss, primo*.

Rail Bang: Hitting the crotch with the edge of the board while falling off.

Rail: Edge of the board.

Raked Over: Pounded by incoming waves while paddling out.

Rag dolled: Tossed around by the force of the currents while underwater.

Reef Break: Wave that breaks as it passes over a coral reef; dangerous to surf.

Re-entry: Rising vertically to the lip and immediately re-entering the wave.

Regular (foot): Riding the board with left foot forward, as opposed to goofy-foot with left foot forward.

Rhino hunting: Going after the really big waves.

Rincon: Good surfing location in Puerto Rico.

Ripping: Extreme moves on a wave; skillfully executed.

Riyuewan: Good surfing location in Sanya, Hainan, China.

Rock Dance: Entering or exiting the surf over rocks.

Rocker: Degree of curve on a board's horizontal profile. Looked at from the side, *rocker* is the degree of curve from fin to nose; flatter or more curved, each has a performance characteristic.

Rolling: Rolling upside down while laying on a board; done while paddling out to pull through an oncoming wave. Also called *turtle roll*.

Rottnest Island: Good surfing location in Western Australia.

Rip / Riptide: Strong current flowing out from the beach; formed by the waves coming onto the beach having to get back out and being confined into a narrow outward flow.

S

Sand Facial: Scraping the face on the bottom after wipe-out.

Sano: San Onofre, location in San Diego County, California.

Santa Catarina: Good surfing location in Brazil.

Sections: Rideable section(s) of a wave.

Selling Buicks: Hurling up the water swallowed during a wipeout; vomiting.

Set: Series of waves.

Shacked: Being barreled.

Shaka: Friendly hand signal with extended thumb and little finger.

Shape: Form of a wave.

Shoot the Curl: Riding through the tubular part of a cresting wave.

Shoot the Pier: Riding between pier pylons.

Shoot the Tube: Riding through the curling part of a cresting wave.

Shore Break / Shorey: Waves breaking close to the beach.

Shoulder: Unbroken section of the wave.

Shove-it / Shuvit: Turning the board through 180 degree half circle, or even 360 full circle and continuing to ride.

Shred: Aggressive surfing.

Shubee/Shubie: Someone who dresses in surf-gear but does not, or cannot surf.

Sick: Good or very good.

Sidewalk Surfing: Skateboarding.

Skeg: Tail fin.

Sketchy: Clumsy surfing technique.

Slash: Radical turn at the top of a wave.

Smack the Lip / Hit the Lip: After a fast bottom turn, moving up fast to the peak.

Snaking: Stealing another surfer's wave; not waiting your turn; often done by paddling around behind the other surfer(s) to get into position.

Snap: Sharp, snappy turn off the top of a wave.

Snapper Rocks: Good surfing location on the Gold Coast, Australia.

Soul arch: Arching one's back while riding a wave; a nonchalant gesture.

Soup: White water from a breaking wave.

Special K: Good surfing location in Samoa.

Spin Out: Wiping out when the tail and fin lose contact with the water.

Spinner: 360-degree turn; full circle spin.

Spit: Spray from the end of a barrel.

Sponger: Body-boarder

Stall: Slowing down by bearing down on the tail and/or dragging a hand in the water; regulate speed to stay in the tube.

Steamer Lane: Good surfing location in Northern California.

Stoked: Pleased, happy.

Stick: Surfboard.

Stringer: Backbone of a surfboard; strip of wood running down the center from nose to tail; gives the fiberglass halves something to hold on to.

Switch-foot: Being able to switch from regular to goofy-foot.

Sucking Dry: When the water in front of a breaking wave is drawn up, exposing the sea bed.

Sultans: Good surfing location in North Male, Maldives.

Sunzal: Good surfing location in El Salvador.

Superbank: Good surfing location on Queensland's Gold Coast, Australia; part a 70 klm (45 miles) stretch of beaches with four excellent point breaks, Superbank being one of them.

Surfari: Surfing adventure; to go looking for good surf.

Surf Bunny: Girl or woman; surfer in her own right, and/or surfer's girlfriend.

Surf Wax: Wax applied to board's deck to improve grip.

Surfer's Knots: Patches of roughened skin on feet and knees from kneeling on the board; callouses caused by deck abrasion over time.

Surf's up: Worthwhile surfing conditions.

Swallow Tail: Surfboard tail resembling a swallow's tail.

Swell: Solid waves rolling in from the deep ocean; as distinct from shallow wind-chop.

Switch Stance: Changing from regular to goofy stance, or vice-versa.

T

Tail: Rear end of surfboard.

Tailside: Slide the tail end across the lip.

Tail Slide: Fin loses grip, board slides sideways.

Taking Gas: Wiping-out.

Take-off: Beginning a ride; catching a wave.

Tandem surfing: Two people on one board; the smaller person is usually held above or stands/sits on the shoulders of the other.

Template: basic shape of a surfboard; what the board is built around.

The Zone: Wave-break zone.

Thruster: Tri-fin short board.

Toes on the Nose: Toes of one or both feet on or hanging over the nose, as in *hang five, hang ten*.

Tofino: Good surfing location in Vancouver Island, Canada.

Tombstone: Surfboard vertical in the water; occurs when surfer is climbing up their own leg-rope to the surface after a wipe-out.

Top Turn: Similar to the re-entry; approach is less vertical, done to gain speed.

Tow in: Being towed out by a jet-ski or other fast agile craft; a necessity with big wave surfing.

Traction Pad: High-grip surface applied to the deck of the board, making surf wax unnecessary.

Trim: Efficient angle while riding a wave.

Tube: Tube formed by the cresting wave.

Tubed: Inside the *tube*.

Tube riding/Getting barreled: Inside the hollow curl of a wave.

Turtle Roll: Longboard technique to get past oncoming waves. Rider lies flat, rolls over before the wave hits, rolls back after wave has passed, paddles on.

Twin Fin : Board with two fins.

U

Ulluwatu: Good surfing location in Indonesia.

V

Val: Valley Girl, resident of the San Fernando Valley; eg. *ok fine, fer sure, fer sure, she's a valley girl and there is no cure* (Frank Zappa).

Valley Boy: Male version of Valley Girl.

Vanuatu: Good surfing location in the South pacific, off the coast of Australia.

W

Wahine: Female surfer.

Walking the Board: Stepping back and forth on the surfboard; done to keep control.

Walking the Nose: Walking up to the nose of the board.

Watergate Bay: Good surfing location in Cornwall, England.

Wax: Waterproof, high grip wax rubbed on the deck of the board to provide a non-slip surface.

Washing Machine: Churned around under a wave after wiping out.

Wedge: Good surfing location in Newport Beach, California.

Wetsuit: Neoprene suit worn against the cold.

White Beach: Good surfing location in Okinawa, Japan.

Whitewater: Turbulent water in the wake of a breaking wave.

Wipe-out: Falling off, being knocked off one's board while riding; wipe-outs can be anything from a mild inconvenience to fatal.

Woodie: Wood-paneled station wagon favored by Californian surfers in the 1960's. Woodies were usually based on old 1940s and '50s wagons, bought cheaply second or third hand.

Worked: Severe wipeout when a surfer is trapped underwater a long time by extreme turbulence or snagged leg-rope; sometimes fatal.

X

(e)Xtreme: Extreme.

Xtrak: Brand of surfboard traction pad.

Y

Yallingup: Good surfing location in Western Australia.

Z

Zog's Sex Wax: Brand of surf wax.

Zipperless: Wet-suit with no zip; lets very little cold water in.

Zonal: The extreme weather in the Southern Ocean around Antarctica is a swell factory that sends big waves half-way around the world. These swells run west-to-east reaching the eastern Pacific coasts of California, Baja and Mainland Mexico, plus Central America.

Zulu: Greenwich Mean Time (GMT). Used on weather charts and read by serious surfers looking for where the best conditions are likely to be.

About The Author

David Tuffley grew up on Brisbane's Southside and the beaches of the nearby Gold Coast. It was here that his love of the surfing lifestyle began and it has stayed with him throughout his life.

Visit David's Websites:

Altiora Publications

David Tuffley's Facebook

David's Amazon Author Page

Other Books for David Tuffley

See David's other books on a wide range of subjects at his <u>Amazon Author Page</u>

One Last Thing...

If you enjoyed this book or found it useful I'd be very grateful if you'd post a short review on Amazon. Your support really does make a difference and I read all the reviews personally so I can get your feedback and make this book even better.

Thanks again for your support!